HAUS CURIOSITIES

Secret Service

About the Contributors

Jonathan Evans was Director General of the British Security Service from 2007 to 2013. In 2018, he was appointed Chair of the Committee on Standards in Public Life.

Claire Foster-Gilbert is the founder director of Westminster Abbey Institute. A public philosopher and author, Foster-Gilbert has played an instrumental role in the fields of medical research ethics and environmental issues.

Edited and with an Introduction by Claire Foster-Gilbert

SECRET SERVICE

National Security in an Age of Open Information

Jonathan Evans

First published by Haus Publishing in 2020
4 Cinnamon Row
London SW11 3TW
www.hauspublishing.com

A CIP catalogue record for this book is
available from the British Library

Print ISBN: 978-1-912208-94-4
Ebook ISBN: 978-1-912208-95-1

Typeset in Garamond by MacGuru Ltd

Printed in Czech Republic

Contents

Acknowledgements

Sincere thanks are due to the Dean and Chapter of Westminster, the Steering Group and Council of Reference of Westminster Abbey Institute, Asha Astley, Ruth Cairns, Dominic Grieve, Harry Hall, John Hall, Peter Hennessy, Alice Horne, Kathleen James, Stephen Lamport, Paddy McGuinness, Seán Moore, Barbara Schwepcke, Mark Sedwill, Vernon White, and Sunbeam House in Hastings.

Introduction

Claire Foster-Gilbert

The following question is a test of integrity: how do I behave when no one is looking? We are not able to watch the spies, our 'secret servants,'[1] who watch us without our knowing (and thereby discover the answer to that very question). It seems reasonable to believe we only behave well if we know we are being watched – witness the vile depths to which anonymous social media posts descend – but the belief is a *reductio ad absurdum*. That would mean those who watch need to be watched themselves, and who will watch the watchers? Doom pictures of the End of Days adorn the eastern walls of some medieval churches, in full view of the congregation, depicting hell with its pitiless treatment of souls who have erred in life. These grim images are at eye level, one notices; while images of heaven, where well-behaved souls bask in God's glory, are painted high up on the wall, near the ceiling – much harder to see, especially without artificial light. Hell's fury acted as a deterrent to medieval bad behaviour: God is watching, and God will call you to account. At least when God was invoked (and the church did not claim divine power for itself) the matter lay between individuals and their consciences. Today, the eyes behind social media are watching, and their piti-less attacks do not wait for the death of their target. Today, we have the rule of law, but there is not enough ink or electronic bandwidth in the world to write the laws that would be needed if we do not, in the end, trust each other to behave well when no one is looking. Trust is necessary if our intelligence services are to do their job.

Transparency in public service can help maintain good behaviour and standards, but it does not create them. Lord Evans asserts that long before the greater transparency expected of today's public servants, including secret servants, there was a code of behaviour within MI5 where he worked for 33 years. In his essay, an edited and updated version of a lecture he gave in Westminster Abbey in 2016, he welcomes a degree of transparency in the service, but he is clear that it is *not* transparency that makes spies behave. Integrity's question of how one behaves when no one is looking is paramount for the intelligence services because their work, by definition, is done under the cloak of darkness. Their integrity comes, Lord Evans argues, from a strong institutional ethos that is internalised by those who work there. As Director General, he knew that the operatives were MI5's greatest strength – but also, at the same time and for the same reason, its greatest weakness: their very ability to gather and analyse information gives them power to serve the public good or damage the service. A senior MI6 operator[2] noticed how demotivated his staff became when they no longer believed in the integrity of a particular operation; by the same token, he saw how overseas intelligence sources were motivated to help British intelligence officers because they felt their own systems were corrupt. So Lord Evans made it his business to attend to their ethical health using both a moral framework and an ethics counsellor.

Intelligence officers must act with integrity, not because someone is watching, nor because of punitive laws, nor through fear of the shame of exposure. Their integrity must be woven into their understanding of their role, be inherent in it, as it is in all professions. A doctor, for example, is not just a person who performs certain skilled functions. A doctor is someone whose duty of care to their patients sits at the heart of their work, and this means they are never truly off duty because at any moment, wherever they are, a member of the public could turn into a patient and be owed that care.

We are unlikely to hear, over an intercom system, 'is there a spy in the house?' and yet there is an equivalent to the doctor's duty of care to their patients for those working in intelligence. And it springs from the particular fact that intelligence officers are privy to information about us, information which gives them power over us, especially as we don't know they have it. Their deepest motivation, resilient enough to withstand the temptation to do otherwise, must be to use that privileged power for the good.

However, one thing that is certain in the world of secret intelligence is that any definition of 'good' is full of compromise. David Omand, who worked for many years at the most senior levels of national security, coined the term 'satisficing' to describe finding a solution that, though not perfect, is adequate to the task in hand.[3] We have a number of fundamental rights that are also moral imperatives: the right to life, to the rule of law, to freedom of speech and assembly, and to the enjoyment of property and privacy. Intelligence officers cannot ensure all of these equally and simultaneously, so we have to 'satisfice' them. But 'satisficing' is of no moral use as a concept if it permits low ethical standards. The concept needs to serve the intention to find the best solution given all the constraints. It requires what Lord Evans calls 'ethical buoyancy', a state where one's moral antennae never cease to vibrate, where moral sensitivity is retained in the face of constantly changing situations and demands for hitherto unthought of responses. The ethical spy, then, must not only desire to serve the common good but also cultivate a habit of finding the best way of doing so in every presenting context and not giving up because the achievable good is a very long way away from perfection.

How is the best way found? This question has been asked by moral philosophers through the ages, and three ways of answering it have emerged: goal-based, duty-based and right-based.[4] Goal-based morality asserts that the action is good if its outcome is good, so our concern is to work out whether that outcome really is desirable and right. Jeremy Bentham suggested a mathematical approach whereby every human counts as 'one', so the greatest good is to be found when the greatest number are made happy or given pleasure.[5] Ensuring that one's goal is morally desirable is the first question, because the goal gives rise to the action itself. We don't usually act without intending a certain outcome – though the goal itself might not be self-evident. It is fascinating to read, in Christopher Andrew's history of intelligence, of the failure of western analysts to understand that Stalin was more concerned with his goal of assassinating Trotsky than he was about the prospect of a Nazi-German attack in the Second World War – even though this was Russia's greatest threat since Napoleon. Nor were Allied minds able to comprehend that Hitler was more obsessed with his goal of the 'Final Solution' than he was with the desperate need for resources on that demanding eastern front.[6]

For British intelligence services today, the uncontroversial, overarching goal of their work is the morally desirable one of the security of all citizens. This goal is determined by our democratically elected government, which in turn directs the agencies to more specific goals, such as the stability of certain states, the suppression of appalling weapons and their use, or the proper deployment of humanitarian assistance. These goals are, or should be, scrutinised by parliament on the public's behalf. They are concerned with the security of all citizens, but they also constitute the moral purpose that the UK has committed itself to in treaty and law.

The goal of security is uncontroversial, but it does not remain so if, with a goal-based mindset, our moral consideration has come to an end simply because our goal is good. Security *is* a good goal, but not at any cost. The limitation of the goal-based approach is that it doesn't question the rightness of the *action* that is being proposed, only what the action will bring about.

Duty-based morality, the second approach, attends to this question. For the duty-based thinker, ends do not justify means: even if the end is morally desirable, the means must be judged on their own moral merits. However desirable my intended outcome might be, is what I have to do to achieve it acceptable? First, the duty-based moralist will ask, are there some actions that can never be justified, that are always simply wrong? We might argue, for example, that it would always be wrong to hide cameras in bathrooms or bedrooms, locations of the most deeply private human actions of all. Or that it is always wrong for an agent to betray someone by starting a relationship with them, or destroying their wellbeing in some other way in order to gain information from them. The UN's Universal Declaration of Human Rights states that *all* human rights can be infringed under certain circumstances except one: the right not to be tortured.[7] Some might argue that even torture is acceptable if the threat is great enough, but these would be goal-based thinkers. Westminster Abbey Institute ran a seminar for sixth formers in which an army major presented the students with this situation: you are in a room on your own with a person whom you have detained because they know the whereabouts of a bomb that is about to explode in the heart of your city. Would you torture that person in order to find out where the bomb is? The sixth formers, pretty much unanimously, decided that they would. The major said that he would not. Why? Because, he said, however much such an incident might lead to appalling loss of life and critical injuries, society would recover from it. Society would not recover, he said, from being one that regarded torture as acceptable. This real-life example (the seminar, not the scenario) is a good demonstration of the difference between goal-based and duty-based thinking, and the need of the former for the latter. The sixth formers changed their minds.[8]

Absolute moral prohibition is important but, in practice, it is much more common for a balance to be struck in any given context if the moral cost is not so much abhorrent as undesirable. It is undesirable to suffer any infringement of privacy, but most of us are willing to suffer some if it means greater security. For the duty-based moralist, because privacy is morally important, it must not lightly be surrendered, and duty-based thinking never makes the mistake of dismissing the questionable action just because I have decided (or governments have decided) that the outcome does, on balance, justify it. Moral cost should never be disregarded lest we start to normalise bad behaviour, with compromised moral standards becoming accepted as inevitable.

Interrogating the means has the additional advantage of raising practical, operational questions about method. Christopher Andrew writes that British intelligence officers in the Second World War questioned reports of new German weapons because they were 'well aware of the danger of sending messages to agents which they might interpret as a request to confirm the weapons' existence', so that any information coming back from those agents would be unreliable – telling the intelligence officers what the agents thought they wanted to hear, not what was true.[9] But, notes Andrew, 60 years later, the CIA failed to exercise similar caution when seeking agent intelligence on Iraqi weapons of mass destruction (WMDs). They instructed their agents to look for and report on what sources were claiming they knew about WMD activities. They, and their British counterparts, did not ask for reports of 'cases in which people, who might have known about them if they were occurring, in fact saw nothing'.[10]

Even if the goal-based moral approach has satisfied itself that the outcomes are good, and the duty-based approach has satisfied itself that the means to reach them are acceptable, what if those on whose behalf the action is proposed do not want it to happen? What if, for example, the intelligence community – or the government to which it is accountable – has decided that a certain level of surveillance is acceptable given security risks, but citizens find it too intrusive? Rights-based morality, our third approach, asks whether those on whose behalf the action is taking place want it to happen. Taken on its own, this approach too is morally flimsy: just because I want something to happen does not mean, morally, that it should. Moreover, just because I want to enjoy untrammelled privacy and freedom, my wish is an ill-educated one if I do not understand the risks: I really may not know what is best for me.

Because we live in a democracy in the UK, the rights-based requirement for consent to decisions and actions taken by government on my behalf is partly met by the ballot box: we can withdraw our vote from those who make decisions we don't like. But this is not enough. The public needs to actively consent to privacy infringements, which means we need good public education on the risks and responsibilities that come with threats to public safety. Do we understand, wonders Omand, that the power to investigate secretly can mean access to pre-emptive intelligence without governments having to resort to 'extreme measures such as crude profiling based on ethnicity or religion, changing the rules of evidence, introducing house arrest or detention without trial for suspects, courts sitting without a jury or new offences such as association with known terrorists'?[11] So transparency – if not about *what* is being investigated then about the parameters of *how* and the reasons *why* – is important. So is consultation to ensure the public feels it has been heard. As Omand notes, an engaged public will be more willing to provide information on suspicious behaviour,[12] and an understanding public will be less likely to allow 'see it, say it, sorted' to descend into the morally abhorrent and discriminatory neighbour-snitching of Hitler's Germany or Stalin's Russia. Statutes seek to help: the Regulation of Investigatory Powers Act 2000 limits the extent to which privacy can be breached, and the Investigatory Powers Act 2016, to which Lord Evans refers directly, updated investigatory powers in the context of the growing importance and reach of cyberspace. The latter effectively rewrote the law of surveillance from scratch in order to fully incorporate all forms of digital intelligence under the rule of law. It seeks to 'explain in detail, more than ever before, what is involved, and what safeguards apply, in the acquisition of digital data, and what the rules are for the retention of digital data for future use'.[13] Dominic Grieve notes that 'it has brought about considerable change in the way the intelligence agencies work because it involved the avowal of a number of practices that were previously secret'.[14]

With a thorough examination of the desirability of the goal, an honest appraisal of the rightness or otherwise of the means to reach that goal, and really good educational reassurance in two-way dialogue with the public, the secret service of our intelligence community can be morally robust. Moreover, because it has given structured consideration to the moral issues at stake, it is better able to give an account of its decisions and actions should it be called upon to do so. Taken together, then, the three approaches to moral thinking can ensure that, broadly speaking, the right questions are being asked and the moral cost of our intelligence services is properly recognised, understood and guarded against. One might imagine the three approaches as a three-legged stool: it will not hold any weight if one of the legs is longer than any of the others but, with legs of equal length, the stool will be quite steady, even on rocky ground. The moral code Lord Evans developed during his time as Director General mirrors the goal-based, duty-based, rights-based approaches as a triadic framework of legality, proportionality and accountability. The framework sits solidly on the three-legged stool.

The 'rocky ground' beneath the stool might well refer to the complex contexts the security services operate in and their own constant redevelopment. The present UK intelligence community consists of: the Security Service – Military Intelligence 5, or MI5 – which is responsible for domestic intelligence and answerable to the home secretary; the Secret Intelligence Service – Military Intelligence 6, or MI6 – responsible for international intelligence and answerable to the foreign secretary; Government Communications Headquarters, or GCHQ, also answerable to the foreign secretary; the intelligence functions within the armed forces and the police; and the cabinet office's intelligence function, which collates and analyses intelligence for government. Though spying has always been part of human societies – accounts in classical literature and the Hebrew Bible attest as much – the current intelligence community evolved much more recently out of the British Secret Intelligence Bureau, which was set up in 1909. Since then, our intelligence services have shifted their means and methods in waves of response to, in turn, the lead up to and nature of the First World War, the Second World War, the Cold War, and now global terrorist threats. Those waves of change, argues Omand, could equally be said to have taken place in response to technological developments. He calls the First World War 'the radio era', when it became possible to look at patterns of radio communication to generate intelligence. The Second World War saw the development of 'the electronic era' where, in Bletchley Park and Dollis Hill, it became possible to encrypt and decrypt communications. The third era, in which we find ourselves now, is the 'cyberspace era'. This era has, says Omand, three contests: i) a technical contest, which involves defending digital infrastructure that is critical to the running of the country's systems; ii) a contest to protect government networks that carry security and classified information; and iii) a moral contest, which counters the use of digital technology to disseminate hostile ideology and the means to undertake terrorist attacks.[15] Omand predicts that the next era will be characterised by near-instantaneous access for analysts to data from quantum computers, and the role of biological developments including cognitive enhancers. He can imagine the analysts 'literally plugged into their computers and databases ... walking through virtual reality representations of visually presented information, like some giant computer game'.[16]

International events have always influenced domestic ones. As a result, MI5's and MI6's spheres of operation overlap – even though, as Lord Evans points out, their modes of working are importantly different. Today, national borders remain the defining structure within which the intelligence services operate, but the world is changing. US political scientist James N. Rosenau wrote: 'Borders still keep out intruders, but they are also more porous. Landscapes are giving way to ethnoscapes, mediascapes, ideoscapes, technoscapes and finanscapes.'[17] Although for now 'territoriality is still a central preoccupation for many people',[18] this nationalistic way of looking at the world and responding to it will need to adapt to face challenges that brook no national boundaries.

Sources and volumes of intelligence have vastly increased in recent years, highlighting the critical importance of analysis and elucidation as well as collection. The following acronyms (in practice used more by military than civilian intelligence) help explain the vast and growing spread of information sources. There are: HUMINT (human intelligence); SIGINT (signals intelligence); IMINT (satellite and photo reconnaissance); ELINT (radar and electronic); MANINT (measurement and signature); and all these, says Omand, are dwarfed by what he coins OSINT (open sources of intelligence) and PROTINT (protected information, that is, personal information about individuals that resides in government and private sector databases).[19] The challenge for the intelligence services is not so much, any more, the gathering of information; it is all there, it seems, waiting to be received. What matters is the elucidation of it, the making sense of it, the seeing patterns in it, and this is a very great challenge indeed, given the amount of information and the mendacity of so much of it.

My introduction began with the question of how we behave when no one is looking. Acting ethically when no one is looking is a necessary condition of integrity and a necessary quality in our intelligence community, both in its institutions and its people. But the exercise of integrity in this secret, morally fraught space has to be wide awake and ever-responsive to new situations, threats and mindsets: how critical has been the need for moral integrity in response to the Covid-19 pandemic, especially in the use of surveillance. Lord Evans' own resilient, unfussy moral integrity shines through his words, as does his wisdom gained from experience and perspective. The lightness and good humour of his tone belie the pressures of the role, which are, at times, significant: often experienced as a gruelling endurance test of unglamorous intelligence work undertaken in a terrifyingly responsible context. As I end my introduction and hand over to Lord Evans himself, I salute him.

Secret Service: National Security in an Age of Open Information

Jonathan Evans

One of the intriguing things about being head of MI5 is meeting the heads of other security and intelligence services throughout the world. You soon learn that there is a crucial distinction between those security chiefs who see it as their job to keep the people safe, and those who see it as their job to keep the president safe from the people. To put it another way, some secret agencies serve their society and some serve their political masters.

In the UK, the position is clear: the role of the secret agencies is to serve the people by protecting them from national security threats such as terrorism and espionage. What's more, operational decisions, such as who is investigated and how, cannot be made by ministers but instead rest with the professional heads of the agencies. National security in Britain today is thus citizen-centric: protecting the citizen from threats that only government capabilities can address. This approach to national security is reflected in the government counterterrorism strategy 'CONTEST', whose stated aim is to ensure that 'people can go about their lives freely and with confidence'.[20] The secret agencies are public servants, not masters, and they are expressly forbidden from acting in the interests of any political party.

We are lucky in this country to have a long tradition of public service which, while not always fashionable, still has real meaning. It is this tradition that the Westminster Abbey Institute seeks to foster and celebrate, and the Institute, in my view, is right to do so. We should celebrate the fact that so many young (and sometimes not so young) people choose to devote their working lives to public service of many sorts. In the same way, we should celebrate the remarkable number of voluntary organisations working for the common good that we are fortunate to have in this country. This same public service ethos lies behind the instinct for balance and accuracy, which is demonstrated in the best of our journalism. We see public service also in the willingness of people to serve in the intelligence and security services. Here, public acknowledgement is necessarily rare, but the demands on the time, ingenuity and, occasionally, courage of members of the agencies can be considerable. This we might call 'secret' public service.

At the heart of this 'secret service' is a rather awkward truth: in order to be able to serve the people effectively, the secret agencies need to keep secrets from the people they serve. This proposition derives from the fact that a small minority of these people are engaged in the very activities that the agencies are fighting against. It is easy to say, in this age of open information, that 'there are no secrets'. It is easy – but it is not true. There are secrets, and it can be vital to the public interest that they remain secret. These are the nation's secrets, not the secrets of a particular organisation. For example, if MI5 and the police are aware of a group's plans to mount a terrorist attack, it is very important that the group does not know that it is under surveillance so it doesn't act precipitately or run away to a safe haven overseas. Investigation must be brought safely and secretly to a point where all the conspirators are known and there is the best prospect of bringing evidence against them in court. Or, again, if an ingenious technique has been discovered that enables the National Crime Agency to identify predatory paedophiles who are streaming live abuse on the dark web, it is in the interests of their potential victims that the existence of that ingenious technique is not publicly revealed. And, more widely, if we believe that the nuclear deterrent is a necessary part of our security against military attack or blackmail, then the whereabouts of our submarines has to remain secret. So, I would contend that there are secrets that it is in the public interest to protect. But this particular facet of the public interest is in contention with other, equally valid, aspects of the public interest, such as the freedom of the media, freedom of information, due accountability and fair and open justice in the courts.

Secrecy is not fashionable at the moment; it provokes suspicion. The current fashion is for transparency and disclosure. Traditional understandings of secrecy and even privacy are changing. Social media and the internet encourage us to share a great deal more information about ourselves, either directly or with our notional consent. Lower levels of trust in established institutions mean that we expect public figures and institutions to do likewise – sharing information, whether that means responding to freedom of information requests[21] or putting their personal tax returns into the public domain (unless you are Donald Trump). This new 'information environment' has had undeniable benefits: child abuse that had been hidden for decades has been revealed; abuse of expenses by parliamentarians was famously exposed – not by auditors or oversight committees, but by a free press. The effectiveness of government policies can be scrutinised in the light of actual evidence rather than conjecture or assertion, and freedom of information is often the tool that enables the media to obtain the evidence needed to undertake this scrutiny. But this is a tricky world for an organisation that needs not only to protect its own secrets but also to intrude into those of others. It is sometimes said that sunlight is the best disinfectant, but how can that work for an institution that *has* to keep secrets?

*

The Security Service that I joined in 1980 was not an institution where the word 'sunlight' sprang readily to mind. Unbelievable as it may sound, it was only two days after I arrived that I realised that I had actually joined MI5. It did not exactly throw wide the doors and welcome scrutiny. The existence of the service was avowed but very little else about it was. Who worked for it? Where were its offices? What was its budget? What did it do? What was its relationship with government? All of these were secret, and yet MI5 was the most open of the three intelligence services! Back then, MI6 was not avowed at all, despite having a big building in Lambeth, and GCHQ was acknowledged only as a research centre for Foreign Office communications. MI5's relations with the media were minimal. The MI5 legal adviser occasionally had lunch with a trusted contact in the broadsheet press, but that was it. Otherwise, press relations were consigned to the 'D-Notice Committee', which maintained a chivalrous arrangement whereby the media voluntarily agreed not to publish damaging information on defence and security matters. (This arrangement still exists, in a modified form, today.) But despite this lack of sunlight, MI5 did not, in my experience, harbour the terrible infections that one might expect. It was a bit fusty; it was a bit old fashioned and maybe not terribly efficient, but I don't think the lack of sunlight led to anything all that much worse than that. The fundamental values of the service were pretty decent, if unspoken, despite the inward-looking culture. So while the sunlight of scrutiny might be a form of disinfectant, it is certainly not the only way to preserve the integrity of an organisation. Something else was keeping people, broadly speaking, on the straight and narrow.

Of course, our secret services today are a great deal more forthcoming than they were. The relationship between the intelligence services and the media, one important aspect of greater openness, has moved on a long way since I joined MI5 over 35 years ago. In many ways, I believe that this relationship has been beneficial to the service, to the media and to the public. In the old days, a vicious cycle sat at the centre of the relationship. The agencies would not communicate with the media and, as a result, the only voices the media heard were those of the ill-informed or ill-intentioned. Consequently, much reporting on intelligence matters was also ill-informed or hostile, and this only reinforced the problem: since the media were ill-informed and hostile, some in the agencies thought, what was the point of talking to them?

There were those, of course, who benefitted from this

stalemate. I can remember reading, as an undergraduate, Chapman Pincher's racy and revelatory book *Inside Story*.[22] Pincher divulged a great deal more about MI5 than was officially admitted. It was Pincher, the veteran spy watcher at the *Daily Express*, who 'revealed' that Sir Roger Hollis had been a Soviet agent. This wasn't factually correct, as later and better-sourced research from the likes of Professor Christopher Andrew demonstrated[23] – but, in those days, not everything that appeared in the *Daily Express* was necessarily true. To end this stalemate between the secret agencies and the media, a degree of trust would be necessary on both sides: on the part of the agencies, trust that it would be possible to share more information with the media without that information being misused or distorted; on the part of the media, trust that the agencies would be honest rather than play manipulative and self-serving games. Essentially, both sides had to recognise that they had a mutual interest in truthful information reaching the public.

The agencies gradually recognised that, in the modern political environment, attempting to maintain total invisibility and inscrutability was no longer a viable strategy. With the death of deference and with increasing suspicion of established organisations, it became important to the agencies that their story, which they considered a good story, be heard by the public. Otherwise, their ability to recruit staff, to win the support of government and to be provided with the tools they needed to do their job would be progressively eroded. At the same time, they had genuine constraints on what they could say, and they held real secrets that it remained in the national interest to keep. The more serious news and media outlets, for their part, had an interest in really understanding the nature of covert national security threats and how the intelligence agencies went about their work of countering those threats. It would only be with this understanding that they could, in turn, keep their readers, viewers or listeners informed. (Spying, of course, has long been of intrinsic interest to the media because it has a whiff of intrigue and excitement about it. I would also mention that it is much easier to get a mention in the media if you call yourself MI5 rather than the Security Service, simply because 'MI5' is short and suits a headline.) And then, as 9/11 and its aftermath propelled the work of the intelligence agencies from the shadows to the top of the news agenda in an unprecedented way, better informed reporting about what had become quite an important bit of government activity became a necessity. Both sides were starting to recognise that the wider public good required them to develop a more mature relationship. Democracy, which it is part of MI5's job to uphold, cannot flourish without a well-informed public. Andrew Marr makes this point well in his book *My Trade*. Without the media, he argues, you are effectively a 'political zero', which is to say that you cannot have a well-founded opinion on what is going on in the world, you cannot be in a position where you can make a clear statement on those issues, and you cannot base your judgement on truth.[24] Today, some people might say that we are in a 'post-truth' environment. But the fact of the matter is that, for our political system to function effectively, we need to have reliable information. Conversely, democracy cannot flourish where insecurity undermines people's willingness to make decisions freely and to exercise their rights. So freedom and democracy require both security and openness.

From the late 1990s, MI5 decided that, instead of having a press office, they would develop relationships with the editors of major national news outlets and with nominated journalists at most newspapers and broadcasters.[25] MI6 and GCHQ soon followed suit. The Intelligence and Security Committee of Parliament[26] (ISC) described this arrangement in the following terms:

> A number of media outlets have a journalist 'accredited' to the Security Service [MI5] and/or the SIS [the Secret Intelligence Service, or MI6]; these journalists are able to contact the Services for guidance. In turn, they are briefed by the Security Service or the SIS about matters relevant to the Services. The agreement between the Agencies and journalists is that all these contacts are off-the-record and must not be quoted directly.[27]

So we find ourselves today in a situation where flows of information from the government's side to the media are much greater than they were and the media know and report a great deal more about the secret world than was the case a generation ago.

This arrangement, of course, has its critics. David Rose, formerly one of the accredited journalists himself, condemned the system in an article in the *New Statesman* entitled 'Spies and their Lies'. He judged the system to be 'gravely damaging for journalists and spooks alike'.[28] It is damaging for journalists, Rose argued, as they open themselves to the risk of manipulation by the agencies, a risk they continue to take because they did not want to lose their access to the information flow. And, he argued, it is dangerous for the agencies because they cannot openly deny false stories and do not benefit from the accountability and sunshine that a more open approach to the press would afford them. The current system also fails the test set by Heather Brook, an investigative journalist and professor of journalism at City University, who insists that real information consists of 'what you can see and what can be tested' and that journalists should approach government in a spirit of scepticism: 'I want to see the evidence'.[29]

Other critics see the current arrangements as potentially corrupting, and a great deal of secrecy still pertains. I agree that too close an alignment between the agencies and the media is not actually in the public interest. Cronyism and back-scratching are invidious. The Leveson inquiry made very clear the problems that can arise when a relationship becomes too cosy.[30] But deep-dyed cynicism about the motives of either side is also corrosive, damaging and just plain wrong. My personal experience is that, in general, the media take a pretty responsible attitude to reporting on our activities. Journalists occasionally stumble upon some piece of information, the publication of which would be genuinely damaging to national security. Normally, if we explain privately why the publication of the information would be damaging, the story is spiked. We cannot insist on this, but there is a shared recognition that the public interest overrides the interests of publication in certain, limited circumstances. Conversely, there have been plenty of very unwelcome and, in our view, misleading stories that we could not argue put national security directly at risk – even though we would very much have preferred them to go away. In these cases, we might try to explain why a story was misleading or unfair, but usually the story appears anyway.

*

Given that the intelligence agencies cannot give a full public account of their activities and that the media have only limited insight into what is going on, other arrangements are needed to provide assurance that the agencies are not getting up to mischief. Such arrangements have developed a great deal in the last twenty years and have been given greater impetus by developments in the Freedom of Information Act 2000, agency engagement with the courts when their intelligence has been used as evidence, and the development of human rights legislation. These public goods have led to a much wider expectation of accountability on the part of the agencies for how they go about their business and how they use their powers – but these same goods have to be held in balance with the needs of security. Just how to achieve this balance has been the subject of debate, dispute and decision in recent years.

The Freedom of Information Act 2000 can empower citizens and help curb abuses of power, but you clearly cannot have an unfettered right of freedom of information while also protecting the necessary secrets of the intelligence agencies. Parliament decided to exclude the intelligence information of the agencies from the scope of the legislation for this very reason. Still, against this background of more demanding disclosure, the need to use intelligence as evidence has led to developments in how to handle secret material in the courts

– and being subject to the law is perhaps the greatest form of accountability.

The position in the criminal courts is generally straightforward: if the prosecuting authorities want to rely on secret evidence then it has to be laid before the court. There is no provision for evidence to be kept secret in the criminal courts. In this case, it has been judged that the fundamental importance of a fair trial trumps any public threat from using undisclosed evidence to prosecute a terrorist or a criminal. I fully support that judgement, despite the occasional frustrations it may cause.

The position in the civil courts, however, is more complex. The courts may accept, in certain circumstances, that it is possible to provide a fair civil proceeding even when some evidence is not visible to one of the parties. This can only happen with the appointment of a 'special advocate' – a specially appointed but vetted lawyer with full access to the relevant material – to represent the interests of the party excluded from seeing the underlying material. The excluded party will still be given a gist of what the evidence is, and the judge retains the duty to ensure that the overall interests of justice are maintained in their court throughout the process. This procedure is controversial and has been challenged, but it has so far been found to deliver justice within a human rights framework.

Accountability is another area of contention. How can agencies be properly accountable for their actions without those actions being made public in ways that would damage the public interest? In addition to the day-to-day relationships between the agencies and their respective government ministers, parliamentarians oversee the secret services through the ISC. Established in 1994, the committee has always operated within the ring of secrecy, but its aim is to assure those outside that ring that the activities of the agencies are properly accountable, effective and well directed, and it has become much more active and powerful over the last two decades. Some media and political commentators enjoy throwing stones at the ISC and complain that it is toothless and has been captured by the system. I note, however, that some of those making such claims do not actually appear to have read very much of what the ISC has said in its recent reports[31] which go into considerable detail about agency operations and, sometimes, agency failings. It is always easy for those looking in from the outside to claim that the system does not work – but that will always be the case if your benchmark is that you want to see all the evidence with your own eyes. In fact, the quantity of material that is available to the courts and oversight bodies in today's digital world is mind-boggling; the problem is just as much how to make sense of the sheer volume as it is obtaining access to it in the first place. Still, the issue with this form of 'accountability by proxy' is that it ultimately requires you, as a member of the public, to rely on some officeholder or committee to look at the evidence on your behalf and tell you if there's anything amiss. This fails what I might call the Heather Brook test of 'I want to see the evidence'.

If you reveal publicly the totality of what the secret agencies do, then they are no longer secret and their value to the public is undermined. If you do not reveal the totality, then you have to place some degree of trust in others whose job it is to ensure that the agencies are doing the right thing. So the question becomes: whom do you trust to look at the evidence on your behalf? Counterintuitively, some polls suggest that people have remarkably high levels of trust in the intelligence agencies despite – or maybe because of – the modest amounts of information available about them.[32] Journalists and politicians, however, though an important part of the accountability system, are not generally seen as trustworthy and independent.[33]

Judges *are* trusted. In recent years, we have relied more and more on judges as the ultimate check and safeguard on government activity and even, occasionally, on public policy. We have exceptionally independent and capable judges in this country who deserve our support and, I may say, that of the Lord Chancellor. But I am rather troubled about the weight we are putting on the judiciary in terms of public trust and the way we run our society. The response to the Investigatory Powers Bill, before it received royal assent in 2016, is instructive in this regard. The bill sought to place considerably more importance on the role of judges in overseeing the use of intrusive powers by the intelligence agencies and the police. Some commentators had been calling for such a change but, as soon as the bill was first published, some of its critics, who had been calling for judicial involvement in the authorisation of 'warrants', retargeted their guns on the judiciary, asking which judges would undertake this new role and whether, by implication, all judges could be trusted to act dispassionately. This implicit questioning of judges' integrity demonstrates the fragility of the system: if the public loses trust in judges, we will be left in a very difficult and exposed position since they are increasingly the last bulwark against cynicism and mistrust across a swathe of public life.

With this panoply of oversight mechanisms, media strategies, court challenges and so on, what space is left for that folk hero, the whistleblower? I would first say that I think the term whistleblower is overused, and I apologise if I sound like an elderly securocrat. If an insider simply reveals secrets, that does not, in my view, make them a whistleblower. To my mind, a whistleblower is an insider who, in good faith, tries to raise concerns through the appropriate channels about activities that they believe to be contrary to the public interest but, unable to do so, reveals that information publicly. The British government has accepted that there may be circumstances in which a member of an agency feels they have come across malpractice and that it is in the public interest that their voice is heard. For this reason, an insider can go to an outside figure, known as the staff counsellor, who is not a member of an intelligence service and who stands outside the management line. (In 2016, for example, this post in MI5 was filled by a former deputy national security adviser in the cabinet office who has never been a member of an intelligence agency.) The staff counsellor can then pass on any concerns, without revealing the source, to the management of the agencies or can escalate them elsewhere in government. With the existence of this approved escalation channel, I can think of very few circumstances indeed where it would be right or necessary for an insider to go public with their concerns. I am thus highly sceptical of the ethical case for whistleblowing on intelligence matters in the UK context. An insider who has access to sensitive material and decides to publish it for money or to settle scores or to further their personal political goals is not blowing a whistle. On the contrary, they are betraying the public trust placed in them and they are misusing public office for personal ends.

The American Edward Snowden is believed by many to have revealed malpractice and abuse of surveillance – relating principally to the US but also to the UK – that needed to be cleaned up. In the UK, he would have been able to express his concerns within the system and not via the media. In fact, as far as the UK is concerned, subsequent enquiries have failed to identify any substantial illegal or unaccountable activity on the part of the British agencies. The best that can be said about Snowden's revelations, in my view, is that they have prompted the British government to publish more information on the agencies' current use of bulk data.[34] But even this has to be set against the damage wrought by the leaks – not only to the agencies' capability to protect the public against terrorism but to law enforcement's ability to protect vulnerable people from serious crime, particularly on the internet. If you ask me, Snowdon has done more harm than good.

Investigative journalism generally has a more positive role than that of a so-called whistleblower. I have often been struck by the similarities between the professions of intelligence and journalism. Spies and journalists share many instincts: to find out something important and interesting; to try to get collateral ('separate confirmatory information') for what you have discovered; to check if it is reliable; to report what you have found out in clear and accurate terms to those who need to know it; and to make sure you protect your sources – because otherwise you won't have any sources next time. In theory, the various ways in which intelligence agencies are formally held to account should mean there is no role for investigative journalism in their accountability but, as we have seen, the formal systems have not always been quick to identify problems. In fact, they have sometimes been very slow to do so. The media have highlighted – sometimes rather late in the day themselves – areas that need to be brought into the open, such as child abuse.

I hope, of course, there are no dark stains of that sort on the agencies' current activities, but I cannot deny that good investigative journalism continues to play a long-stop role in checking potential abuse. There are risks in publishing unauthorised stories about the agencies, including legal risks to the publisher, but that is the price you pay for a free media and, in my view, it is one that is worth paying. You only need to visit a country where the media are not free to see how dull a compliant media can be, and it tends to go hand in hand with bad government.

*

With all these safeguards in place, it seems hard to believe that the Security Service of the 'old days' was not an organisation rife with corruption and malpractice, even though it was extremely – probably excessively – secretive. The reason seems to be a mixture of culture, ethics and behaviours. Most people join the secret services because they want to serve the public. No doubt the same is true of many who go into the news media. Organisations do well to select people with this motivation and, through their behaviour, organisations can either reinforce this wish to serve or inadvertently erode it. When I joined MI5, there was a largely unspoken set of assumptions about how you should behave and, in my experience, it was broadly healthy and helped protect the service from the dangers that can arise from undue secrecy.

The increasing diversity of views today means that a more explicit articulation of values is needed. The Westminster Abbey Institute refers to these as 'moral and spiritual values'. British public service values, dating at least as far back as the Northcote–Trevelyan report of the nineteenth century,[35] are rooted in Britain's Christian tradition – but they are by no means exclusively Christian in their appeal or application. These values need not only to be articulated but also to be discussed, tested and applied. In my experience, most people – and certainly those you would want to employ in professions such as intelligence or journalism – actively welcome discussions of the ethical problems and dilemmas they face. They are right to do so: open discussion is itself an important element in maintaining an organisation's 'ethical buoyancy', as one senior MI5 colleague has described it. In fact, engaging in such discussion should be seen as one of the responsibilities of those in these jobs. However much oversight or accountability you have, whatever your editorial policy, you cannot prepare everyone for every eventuality. At some point, individual intelligence officers will have to make important judgement calls for themselves and, if we are to trust them to do this, they need to have internalised the values on an individual level, and not just because they have been taught about them but because they believe them. This is as true of the media as it is for the intelligence agencies and for many other professions. When I was the director of a bank, I saw the same issues played out in that world: what we care about, what we value and how we measure success will have an impact on the critical decisions we make for better or worse. Individual moral judgement will remain the vital core of a healthy and sustainable organisation.

At the heart of my remarks is the inherent tension between good, inquisitive journalism on the one hand and the instincts and genuine concerns of the secret state on the other. Building trust between the two sides has taken time. But a degree of trust now exists, based on a shared recognition of where the public interest lies and a shared recognition that the values that matter for both sides are, in fact, fundamentally aligned. It would be in the interests of neither side for the relationship to become too close, but it would benefit neither side – nor, more importantly, the public, who are the beneficiaries of the news media and of the efforts of the intelligence agencies – if the two sides were to revert to the trench warfare that prevailed forty years ago.

The Very Reverend Dr John Hall
Thank you very much, Lord Evans. If I may ask the first question: you've talked about accountability through the conventional media and the scrutiny that is given through parliament and so on, but most of us know about you only informally – through novels and films and television programmes. These sources suggest that there is rivalry between MI5 and MI6, and between our intelligence services and those of the United States. Are they right?

Lord Evans

Nothing could be further from the truth! There may well be rivalry between the British services and the Russian services, and I hope that remains the case in view of Russian behaviour. The fact of the matter is that, in practical terms, the relationship between the British agencies themselves, and also between the British agencies and the police, is closer and more collaborative, I would say, than that in any other country that I have ever had anything to do with, bar none. Having said that, of course, the different agencies have slightly different roles and they have slightly different cultures. If you are in MI6, then essentially you are likely to be working in small teams, probably in other countries and on occasion acting without the consent of your host government. In MI5, you are working within a domestic environment and therefore you don't bend the rules in those sorts of ways. That leads to a slightly different corporate culture within the two organisations. There is definitely a degree of friendly joshing and rivalry between the agencies. We enjoy our caricatures of each other but actually, in practical terms, we have a more integrated system here than ever before. I have personal friendships with previous heads of MI6 and also GCHQ, so the impression of rivalry in the sense you imply is quite wrong.

Audience member

As I look at the insanity of [the Brexit referendum in] 2016, there seems to be a narrative of intolerance, hostility, fear and suspicion. There's a danger that, if you are open about threats to national security, you are feeding that fear. Is there a moral or ethical responsibility of MI5 and the other security and intelligence agencies, when they expose secrets, to contribute to a counter-narrative that offers something like optimism and, if it's not too romantic, the idea of hope?

Lord Evans
I haven't been asked that question before and it's an interesting one. There is a suspicion, I know, that when intelligence chiefs speak, their intention is to frighten the public because they've got some desire to extract more money from the Treasury. That has not been the intention. There's a delicate balance to be maintained between, on the one hand, being frank and open (as far as one can) about the reality of the threats that we face and, on the other hand, giving assurance (again, where we can) about the coverage of those threats and the fact that actually, in the UK, we are lucky in having quite an effective counterterrorism system involving not just the agencies but many others. So, I think we need to give a balanced account of the situation that we're in and not just portray bad news. To some extent, of course, that relies also on commentary from others outside the agencies, particularly that of government ministers. I can remember, in the early days of the Cameron government, being asked by a very senior minister at my third meeting with him whether I ever brought good news. Of course, on the whole, the agencies do tend to be looking at not such good things. As a CIA friend of mine said, the trouble with intelligence officers is that when we smell roses, we look for the funeral. He was not entirely wrong. I think what we need to do, as far as we can, is to give a neutral professional assessment both of the downside and the upside of any disclosure we make. I don't think we ought to engage too widely

on policy issues and the wider issues of society because we are here as professionals in one particular area, not as politicians. But I do accept that there is a responsibility not to instil or increase fear.

Audience member

Could I ask about information warfare and hybrid warfare coming from abroad that target our whole society? How much should the intelligence services disclose about the measures they need to take to counter them?

Lord Evans

There are undoubtedly states that are using information, sometimes in a very misleading way, in order to try and influence and take forward their particular political policies overseas. The extent to which you reveal what you know about that is a difficult judgement, because you don't want to betray your own sources. I do think it's been helpful that, in the last few years, statements by GCHQ, the British Government and particularly by the American agencies[36] have identified activities that would have otherwise remained covert. That's a necessary part of informing the public. Nevertheless, there have to be strict constraints on what they can disclose.

Audience member

When there is a conflict between the public good and, perhaps, what is lawful, or pressure from government, how does MI5 find its moral compass?

Lord Evans

I can remember very few occasions when there has been significant pressure on the agencies, in my experience at least, to do things that they did not believe it would be right or lawful to do. It's very risky, in our system, for a minister to push officials to do something illegal. Also, there are safeguards, because ministers don't actually have their hands directly on the operational levers. This means that there has to be a relationship of trust between a secretary of state and the agency head in order to ensure that any potentially conflicting issues are effectively managed. I worked directly for four home secretaries and we never got into a position where there was a real stand-off on a question of what was right or lawful. We should be encouraged by this, because it shows how carefully ministers generally discharge their responsibilities in relation to the intelligence services. In my time in the service, we also did some work on creating an ethical framework to direct our moral compass. We consulted moral philosophers and other academics, as well as people in industry. We articulated three simple concepts that underpinned what we saw as our ethical framework: legality, proportionality and accountability. These three principles provide a useful framework with which to address ethical questions – not to give you an easy answer, but to frame your discussion about what is right.

There may sometimes appear to be short-term tactical advantages in acting illegally, for example when engaging with some agencies overseas whose own activities are falling very well short of our own. But the longer-term interest is in acting lawfully. I think that people would be surprised at how much care is taken over these sorts of decisions.

Audience member

Would more sunlight have helped protect the UK against Blunt, Philby, Maclean or Blake?[37]

Lord Evans

I guess it would actually, yes. I think those particular cases were not just to do with the culture and behaviours of the intelligence services; they also arose from deeper issues about the way society perceived itself, from controversies dating back to the 1930s, at a time after the First World War when there was a certain revulsion with the way the world was. Also, the closed world of the agencies reflected wider societal norms. But still, I suspect greater openness would have led to the problems being identified and outed more quickly.

Audience member

I come from a country where there is only one security agency. What would you say would be positive and what would be negative about a merger of the three British secret agencies?

Lord Evans

I don't support a merger. It's what we used to characterise as 'the KGB model'. I think a degree of specialisation in capabilities and culture is valuable. And I think having a single agency would make it difficult to accommodate those different cultures and capabilities, which are needed for the variety of tasks. There is also an issue of accountability. To whom would such an agency report? The home secretary would not deal with foreign issues, nor the foreign secretary with domestic ones. The cabinet office would be unlikely to be able to specialise as would be needed.

It is probably better not to have one huge and potentially over-mighty agency in the UK. I think we are better to have these particularly intrusive powers spread more widely, not concentrated in one place.

Audience member
Would you comment on what I think was one of the most memorable agency-political moments: when Lady Manningham-Buller, in her maiden speech in the House of Lords, made it clear that, from the point of view of her experience in the security services, lengthening the time for which people could be held without charge would be counterproductive. As far as I'm aware, she didn't reveal anything that was secret, but she certainly used her experience to very great political effect.

Lord Evans
I was the Director General when Lady Manningham-Buller said that. I'm happy to report that she didn't tell me in advance she was going to say it, which was helpful in protecting me from any fallout. I think she did exactly the right thing, which is to use her experience and her judgement as a cross-bench peer to inform the debate of the Upper House. I think her intervention was very influential, and it demonstrates the value of having somebody of her stature who is willing to speak out on these issues.

Audience member
You referred to the cultural differences between the agencies. You haven't talked at all about the relationship between the agencies and the military intelligence and security activity

that complements all of them. I live in a country, Israel, where there's a great deal of interplay between the agencies and with the military, including secondment of people at different levels from one agency to another for different periods of time. Do you think that this is something that would be valuable for the intelligence and security world? Would you also comment on the role of the agencies in educating politicians in the role of intelligence and security?

Lord Evans

In the Israeli system, of course, military intelligence is a much bigger player on a day-to-day basis than is the case in the UK. But obviously, in Britain, military intelligence is still extremely important in ensuring that our armed forces are well informed and can deliver the correct capabilities to the right places. They don't have a big role in domestic security for all sorts of constitutional and other reasons, but there is a friendly relationship between the civil agencies and the military intelligence community. Of course, in times of war, there are arrangements for optimising intelligence support to live operations.

Interplay between the agencies is crucial. One of the good things that we developed on the counterterrorism side was that, in my stations across the UK, we had MI6 officers present who were able to bring their experience and expertise. Equally, in some of the critical posts overseas, I had officers working for MI6 in their stations, and I think that was helpful to both sides. And the same with GCHQ. The same applies, actually, to the police; we have a similar close working relationship with the Metropolitan Police and regionally. Certainly, MI5 view the police as being an enormous asset to us, because here you have a body of world-class detectives and police officers who are able to take difficult cases and turn them into prosecutions and get the bad guys off the streets.

I'll just make one comment on the education of politicians. I think it's really important that the agencies continue to provide non-partisan briefings for the Leader of the Opposition and key opposition ministers so that the those in opposition understand the issues. Generally, government has been very happy for that to be the case, and I think it ensures a more mature debate on these issues and also ensures that, if you do get a change of government, you have not got a group of incoming ministers who have no knowledge of intelligence matters.

Audience member

From the point of view of information, does the intelligence community pay any attention to *Russia Today* operations, or is it entirely inconsequential?

Lord Evans

I think you'd have to be an extremely naive consumer of news not to realise that *Russia Today* is a biased Russian front that is pushing out propaganda. I don't think the government needs to do a lot about that, because it is self-evident. In a sense, if it's just *Russia Today* that's pumping out propaganda, that's fine. The problem is when the propaganda is being dressed up and pumped out through other channels, and that can also happen. A variety of countries have tried that over the years. So I think the bigger risk is where there is covert activity, rather than straightforward and obvious propaganda.

Audience member
To what extent will UK national security be damaged by Brexit?

Lord Evans
My views on Brexit are publicly known. I believe it is not in the British security interest to pull out of the European Union for two reasons. The first one is that, although intelligence cooperation will continue between the UK and European partners and I'm sure will continue at a strong level, there is significant advantage to the UK in being able to be at the table when European policy, which is relevant to national security, is being decided, since it will affect us. It is better for us to be influential in contributing our views when European legislation is being considered rather than just having to accept it when it arrives. It will have an impact on us even if we're not in the EU. And secondly, I think the overall stability and security of Europe has been underpinned by the political structures of the EU, despite their many problems. The fact that the EU is there and that it enables people to cooperate and to work together has, in my view, been a strategically beneficial move and I think that our departure, particularly if it leads to others departing in due course, would raise rather than reduce the security risks to Europe, and we can't isolate ourselves from that because it will affect us.

Audience member
Would you comment on the news that the CIA was seeking the help of Apple for intelligence purposes? How might it have turned out if it had happened in the UK?

Lord Evans

It was a very public and quite an interesting showdown, solved as I understand it by clever Israeli technology which got into the iPhone without having to worry about Apple helping. There are two public goods in conflict here: there is the need to get hold of information about potential terrorism and other national security threats on the one hand and, on the other, there is the fact that it is in the overall national security interests of the UK and other countries for there to be effective cybersecurity in order to reduce risks in cyberspace. So it is a question of how you hold those in tension. The Investigatory Powers Act 2016 addresses this issue as it provides, effectively, legislation to allow the intelligence agencies and the police to engage with technology companies to see where there are opportunities to access information collaboratively and under statute. But the Act does not intend, wholesale, to put backdoors into cryptography. I think that's probably about as good a deal as we can get. It's important to maintain the security of communications more widely and therefore opening too wide a gap in the defences would seem to me to be counterproductive – but it's an unresolved issue.

The Very Reverend Dr John Hall

Lord Evans, I want to take this opportunity, if I may, to thank you twice. Once for your work with the Security Service. We're all immensely conscious of the benefit we receive from the intelligence services and the extraordinarily important work they do. It is a risky and difficult business, so thank you and, through you, could we thank others involved in your extremely important work. And thank you for your generous exposition tonight. It's been a very enlightening time. Accountability is vital to the integrity of public service and you have been very open in your account to us of our secret services.

Postscript

Jonathan Evans

My talk and the subsequent Q&A date from the period between the UK's EU referendum in June 2016 and the inauguration of President Trump the following January. Since then, there have been developments in a number of the areas that I touched on – some, but not all, in a negative direction.

The overall security situation has deteriorated since 2016. There were the terrorist attacks in London and Manchester in 2017; the rise in extreme right-wing terrorism, which is now recognised as a national security threat; the Russian state's use of chemical weapons on the streets of Salisbury; and a continued rise in abuse and intimidation aimed at those in elected office, their families and staff, and at some public officials. Consequently, the pressures on the security and police services have remained intense at a time when the tone of political debate has become harsher and more divisive, established political and constitutional norms have been challenged, and support for the rule of law and the judicial process have been muted – including from some ministers, whose responsibility it is to support them.

In my talk, I refer briefly to the issue of what constitutes truth in the public arena. There has been intense public debate, and quite intense public concern, about this issue in the intervening period. Traditional 'media gatekeepers' are losing power, and populist political leaders no longer feel constrained by assumptions about how politicians should communicate. Some leaders appear to have a hazy notion of the distinction between truth and wishful thinking, and others judge that well-informed public debate and challenge are actively unhelpful to their cause. This apparent drift away from evidence-based policymaking and the subordination of facts to ideology poses a particular challenge to the intelligence services. We now know, for example, that President Trump sought the personal loyalty of FBI director James Comey rather than recognising his necessary political neutrality. Similarly, if facts are subordinated to ideology and political advantage, then the role of the agencies in 'telling truth to power' can be characterised as treachery rather than professionalism. If you already believe you know the truth as a result of your ideological insights, then why do you need the complex and expensive apparatus of an intelligence community to help inform you? I am aware of no evidence that these problems have so far presented themselves in the UK, but the decrying of experts because they do not support your political ideology and the complaint that judges are 'enemies of the people'[38] have a flavour of the same mindset.

In both the lecture and in my answers to audience questions, I mention the way in which social media can be manipulated by governments for political ends. More information on this has been revealed in the Mueller investigation into Russian interference in US politics.[39] In the UK, the Cambridge Analytica scandal has shown that the cynical misuse of social media data is not just a tool of state conflict but can also be used to achieve effects in domestic politics. But, at the same time, the last three years have seen a much wider public recognition of the risks inherent in the power of big technology companies. This, in turn, has led the companies themselves to recognise that it is in their own interests to acknowledge a degree of social responsibility for how their platforms are being used if they are to continue to be seen by their users as a benign rather than a sinister force. The British government has taken this a step further by proposing a much tighter regulatory regime to counter what it calls 'online harms'.[40] Along with the implementation and global reach of European data protection legislation, it appears that, over time, at least in the democratic world, public and market pressure might lead to a rebalancing of power between the big technology companies and the citizen in favour of the public interest.

My characterisation of the relationship between the intelligence community and the media, which has played an important part in helping the agencies adapt to a more open society, relied quite heavily on the relationship between the agencies and the traditional media outlets. In today's rapidly changing world, this relationship remains important but addresses only part of a much wider media spectrum. Managing your engagement with the public only through traditional media looks increasingly inadequate. Opinions and judgements are still influenced by traditional journalism, but its near monopoly of public debate has gone. This shift poses a challenge to the intelligence agencies, much of whose work does not lend itself to regular tweeting and interactive discussion.

It has been striking the extent to which GCHQ in particular has taken a much higher public profile in the last few years, largely through its outreach relating to cybersecurity, an area of concern for both ordinary citizens and companies. Cybersecurity is an area where there is a lot that can and should be said publicly and where the value of public communication is clear. GCHQ's involvement in helping people and businesses go about their lives and work safely has proved an ideal basis for demonstrating the value of this agency's work and underpinning trust in what it does. Finding a similar platform for maintaining public trust in the remainder of the work of the intelligence community, without exposing information that undermines the work itself, will continue to require careful but innovative steps in the coming period.

January 2020

Notes

1   Spies are 'watched' by means of ministerial, Commissioner and parliamentary oversight, but the process of authorising, conducting, supervising and regulating covert intelligence activities is undertaken in secret. There is also internal professional accountability, but again, this happens in secret.

2   Paddy McGuinness, former Deputy National Security Adviser, personal communication, February 2020.

3   David Omand and Mark Phythian, *Principled Spying: The Ethics of Secret Intelligence* (Oxford, Oxford University Press, 2018) pp. 144–145.

4   For a longer discussion of the three moral approaches, see my essay 'Moral Analysis' in Claire Foster-Gilbert (ed.) *The Moral Heart of Public Service* (London, Jessica Kingsley Publishers, 2017) pp. 43–59.

5   Jeremy Bentham, 'An Introduction to the Principles of Morals and Legislation' in Mary Warnock (ed.) *Utilitarianism* (Glasgow, William Collins Sons and Co, 1962, originally published 1789) pp. 33ff.

6   Christopher Andrew, *The Secret World: A History of Intelligence* (London, Penguin, 2019) p. 743.

7   Omand and Phythian, op. cit. p. 30.

8   A former intelligence officer in the army noted: 'We also don't employ torture because as a general rule

it doesn't work, or at least other methods can work equally well without having to resort to crimes against humanity. My personal experience of conducting interrogations in Abu Ghraib prison in 2003 was that you can get a lot more out of a detainee by giving him a cup of tea and a phone to speak to his family than through "enhanced interrogation techniques".

9   Andrew, op. cit. p. 741.
10 Ibid. pp. 740–741.
11 David Omand, *Securing the State* (London, Hurst and Company, 2010) p. 108.
12 Ibid. p. 111.
13 Omand and Phythian, op. cit. p. 151.
14 Dominic Grieve, former Chair of the Intelligence and Security Committee of Parliament, personal communication, February 2020.
15 Omand and Phythian, op. cit. pp. 113ff.
16 Ibid. p. 117.
17 Quoted in Omand and Phythian, op cit. p. 14.
18 Ibid.
19 Omand, op. cit. p. 120.
20 The Home Office, *CONTEST: The United Kingdom's Strategy for Countering Terrorism* (London, TSO, 2011) available at https://assets.publishing.service.gov.uk/government/uploads/system/uploads/attachment_data/file/97995/strategy-contest.pdf, accessed 16th January 2020. David Omand, when he was Security and Intelligence Coordinator, launched the strategy and coined the acronym: COuNter-TErroism STrategy (Omand, op. cit. p. 80).

21 The Freedom of Information Act 2000 grants, and also limits, the right to access to information held by Public Authorities.

22 Chapman Pincher, *Inside Story: A documentary of the pursuit of power* (London, Sidgwick & Jackson, 1981).

23 Christopher Andrew, *The Defence of the Realm: The authorised history of MI5* (London, Penguin, 2009).

24 Andrew Marr, *My Trade: A short history of British journalism* (London, Pan, 2005) p. 381.

25 This was in addition to explaining themselves more openly through booklets and the occasional public utterance by the heads of agencies.

26 The Intelligence and Security Committee has statutory oversight of the UK intelligence community. It was established by the Intelligence Services Act 1994 (governing MI6 and GCHQ), with powers reinforced by the Justice and Security Act 2013 (governing the whole of the Security Service), tasking the Committee with statutory responsibility for oversight of the intelligence community.

27 Intelligence and Security Committee, *Annual Report 2004–5* (London, HMSO, 2005) p. 31, available at http://isc.independent.gov.uk/committee-reports/annual-reports, accessed 29th January 2020.

28 David Rose, 'Spies and their Lies' in *New Statesman* 27th September 2007, available at https://www.newstatesman.com/politics/2007/09/mi6-mi5-intelligence-briefings, accessed 16th January 2020.

29 Personal communication.

30   Department for Digital, Culture, Media and Sport, *The Leveson Inquiry: Report into the culture, practices and ethics of the press* (London, TSO, 2012) available at https://www.gov.uk/government/publications/leveson-inquiry-report-into-the-culture-practices-and-ethics-of-the-press, accessed 16th January 2020.

31   See e.g. International and Security Committee, *Report on the Intelligence Relating to the Murder of Fusilier Lee Rigby* (London, HMSO, 2014), available at http://isc.independent.gov.uk/committee-reports/special-reports, accessed 29th January 2020.

32   This is according to unpublished polling conducted by Ipsos Mori.

33   Ipsos Mori, 'Veracity Index 2019: trust in professions survey', Ipsos MORI Social Research Institute report, available at www.ipsos.com, accessed 17th January 2020.

34   The UK government made these changes in the context of the Investigatory Powers Act 2016.

35   Stafford H. Northcote and C.E. Trevelyan, *Report on the Organisation of the Permanent Civil Service* (London, HMSO, 1854).

36   For example, in evidence submitted to the Public Bills Committee on the Investigatory Powers Bill, 2016.

37   These four, along with John Cairncross, formed the so-called 'Cambridge Five' spy ring. As British government employees, they passed secret information to the Soviet Union between the 1930s and 1950s.

38   Headline in the *Daily Mail* 4th November 2016.

39   Robert S. Mueller III, *Report on the Investigation into Russian Interference in the 2016 Presidential Election*

(Washington, DC, US Department of Justice, 2019), available at www.justice.gov/storage/report.pdf, accessed 29th January 2020.

40 Department for Digital, Culture, Media and Sport, *Online Harms* (London, DCMS White Paper, 2019).

WESTMINSTER ABBEY INSTITUTE

Secret Service in an Age of Open Information is published in partnership with Westminster Abbey Institute. The Institute was founded by Westminster Abbey in 2013 to work with the people and institutions by whom it is surrounded in Parliament Square, to revitalise moral and spiritual values and virtues in public life. It offers space and time for challenging lectures, conversations, ideas and quiet reflection.

In doing so, the Institute aims to remind those who govern of their vocation to public service, helping them to grow in moral sensitivity and resilience and to better define the good they are trying to do.

The material in this book does not necessarily represent the views of Westminster Abbey or its Institute.

HAUS CURIOSITIES

PUBLISHED WITH WESTMINSTER ABBEY INSTITUTE

The Power of Politicians
by Tessa Jowell and Frances D'Souza

The Power of Civil Servants
by David Normington and Peter Hennessy

The Power of Judges
by David Neuberger and Peter Riddell

The Power of Journalists
by Nick Robinson, Gary Gibbon,
Barbara Speed and Charlie Beckett

The Responsibilities of Democracy
by John Major and Nick Clegg

Integrity in Public Life
by Vernon White, Claire Foster-Gilbert and Jane Sinclair

HAUS CURIOSITIES

Inspired by the topical pamphlets of the interwar years, as well as by Einstein's advice to 'never lose a holy curiosity', the series presents short works of opinion and analysis by notable figures. Under the guidance of the series editor, Peter Hennessy, Haus Curiosities have been published since 2014.

Welcoming contributions from a diverse pool of authors, the series aims to reinstate the concise and incisive booklet as a powerful strand of politico-literary life, amplifying the voices of those who have something urgent to say about a topical theme.

'Nifty little essays – the thinking person's commuting read' – *The Independent*

Britain in a Perilous World: The Strategic Defence and Security Review We Need
by Jonathan Shaw

The UK's In-Out Referendum: EU Foreign and Defence Policy Reform
by David Owen

Establishment and Meritocracy
by Peter Hennessy

Greed: From Gordon Gekko to David Hume
by Stewart Sutherland

The Kingdom to Come: Thoughts on the Union Before and After the Scottish Referendum
by Peter Hennessy

Commons and Lords: A Short Anthropology of Parliament
by Emma Crewe

The European Identity: Historical and
Cultural Realities We Cannot Deny
by Stephen Green

Breaking Point: The UK Referendum
on the EU and its Aftermath
by Gary Gibbon

Brexit and the British: Who Are We Now?
by Stephen Green

These Islands: A Letter to Britain
by Ali M. Ansari

Lion and Lamb: A Portrait of British Moral Duality
by Mihir Bose

Drawing the Line: The Irish Border in British Politics
by Ivan Gibbons

Not for Patching: A Strategic Welfare Review
by Frank Field and Andrew Forsey

A Love Affair with Europe: The Case for a European Future
by Giles Radice

Fiction, Fact and Future: The Essence of EU Democracy
by James Elles

We Are the People: The Rise of the AfD in Germany
by Penny Bochum